POLYNESIAN CULTURAL CENTER
All the spirit of the islands. All in one place.

T E X T   B Y   R I T A   A R I Y O S H I

A Polynesian Welcome

▲▲▲▲▲▲▲▲▲▲▲▲▲▲▲▲▲▲▲▲▲▲▲▲▲▲▲▲▲▲▲▲▲▲▲▲▲▲▲

TALOFA *(tah-LOW-fah)*—SAMOA

IA ORA *(key-ah-OH-rah)*—AOTEAROA (New Zealand)

BULA VINAKA *(boo-lah-vee-NAH-kah)*—FIJI

ALOHA *(ah-LOW-ha)*—HAWAI'I

KAOHA *(kah-OH-ha)*—MARQUESAS

IA ORA NA *(ee-ah-oh-RAH-nah)*—TAHITI

MALO E LELEI *(mah-low-eh-leh-LEH-ee)*—TONGA

NO MATTER HOW IT'S SAID, IT MEANS WELCOME —welcome to the Polynesian Cultural Center, 42 acres of Pacific Island experience–the real thing. "The loveliest fleet of islands that lies anchored in any ocean," Mark Twain said of Hawai'i but he might have been referring to all the Polynesian islands. Robert Louis Stevenson, Jack London, Herman Melville, Somerset Maugham, James Michener, and a host of other famous writers all agreed and fell in love with Polynesia. Sailors who discovered these alluring islands succumbed to their charms and never went home. Millions of visitors have passed through the thatched portals of the Polynesian Cultural Center, discovered the same beauty and excitement, and have been just as reluctant to leave.

In the town of Laie on Oahu's north shore, The Church of Jesus Christ of Latter-day Saints founded the Center in 1963 next to the Church College of Hawai'i so students could work their way through college by sharing their island heritage with visitors. Today the Church College of Hawai'i is the Hawai'i campus of Brigham Young University. The students come from an area that covers approximately 15 million square miles of the world's largest ocean—the Pacific. Most of the Polynesian islands lie within a triangle marked by Hawai'i at the northern apex, Easter Island in the southeast, and New Zealand in the southwest. Seven of

C O N T E N T S

ISBN 0-9644640-0-4

these island nations are represented at the Polynesian Cultural Center.

At the heart of the Polynesian experience are the island villages which offer the visitor a special opportunity to learn about the language and customs of each island, its arts and crafts, architecture, foods and dress. Visitors are encouraged to take part in a number of activities, unique to the Polynesian islands, and to get to know some of its people on a one-to-one basis. The daily shows, featuring the songs and dances of the islands, are the highlight of a visit to the Polynesian Cultural Center. All-you-can-eat buffets, a canoe pageant, shops, canoe rides and an optional tour of nearby Laie, are all part of the experience.

The fantasy of the islands suggests swaying palms, mysterious green mountains alive with waterfalls, embraced by long stretches of sandy beach, and surrounded by turquoise seas that sparkle in everlasting sunshine. That's the dream. The reality is remarkably similar. There are some rainy days, even in paradise, but there are always rainbows and sunshine just around the corner.

The Polynesian Cultural Center—with its lagoon-laced landscaping, waterfalls, lush tropical flora, and an "erupting" volcano–captures the romance and fantastic beauty of the ocean islands. A day at the Center is a warm and memorable experience, a chance to travel to seven islands of Polynesia in a single day, and participate in the celebration of centuries of Polynesian culture—no passport required.

The Polynesian environment was integral in the daily lives of Polynesians–bathing in shady pools, collecting coconuts in forest plantations, fording streams to visit neighboring villages, gathering leaves for family feast decorations, and picking flowers for personal adornment.

An Hour's Drive–Another World

▲▲

The Polynesian Cultural Center serves the Laie community in many ways: sponsoring educational scholarship programs, offering cultural performances from throughout the Pacific, promoting local beautification efforts, contributing to the fulfillment of academic studies of university students from throughout the world.

IN BUSTLING LEEWARD OAHU, THE VIBRANT CITY OF HONOLULU SERVES AS HAWAII'S capital and is well known for its glittering international resort, Waikiki. Across the Ko'olau mountains to quiet Windward Oahu, just one hour and a world apart, lies the Polynesian Cultural Center on the beautiful North Shore. ◆ The choice of site is significant. In ancient times, Laie was a *pu'uhonua*, a place of refuge. A person accused of trespassing against another was given an opportunity to earn forgiveness. He would be released from captivity, and if he made it to the *pu'uhonua* before his pursuers, he would make atonement to the priests and be forgiven. Laie was also a sanctuary for women and children during times of war. It is hallowed ground. ◆ Blessed with sunshine, cooled by tradewinds, and tended by patient, hard-working people, this corner of Hawai'i duplicates the splendid natural beauty of the scattered homelands of Polynesia.

◄ POLYNESIAN CULTURAL CENTER LAIE

•KANEOHE

•HONOLULU

3

EONS AGO, THE GREAT PACIFIC OCEAN ERUPTED IN FLAMES–AND POLYNESIA WAS BORN. Volcanic sea mounts built these islands, layer upon layer, eruption after eruption, until the gift of land emerged from the depths of the sea. The volcanoes continued their work of creation making mountains high enough to catch the rain clouds–and even snow. Protective coral reefs formed around the islands. The wind, waves and birds brought seeds and the new land became green.

The oldest of these islands have been reclaimed by the ocean, leaving behind only reefs, a range of atolls, and sand washed beaches. The newest are still being born in flames.

Lava outpourings from these ancient volcanic eruptions have created a dramatic coastline of black rocky promontories invading long stretches of golden sandy beaches. Foam-crested waves endlessly roll in, calling surfers from around the world to test their skills. The North Shore is an area of small towns, farms, orchid nurseries, sugar plantations, country people and a way of life still centered around the philosophy of aloha, or love and hospitality towards strangers. It is an ideal setting in which to celebrate the honored cultures of the many islands of Polynesia.

The growth of Laie began with humble beginnings and with each new dedication of significant institutions, it has become a gathering place for spiritual, educational, economic and cultural excellence in the Pacific.

Two-Way Education

In one of the happiest arrangements ever envisioned—and better yet, made into reality—the Polynesian Cultural Center is how thousands of students have worked their way through college.

Getting Started

With missionary zeal and royal pomp, a chapel of The Church of Jesus Christ of Latter-day Saints at Laie was dedicated in 1883. For that occasion, King David Kalakaua sailed with his retinue from Honolulu along the coastline, anchored in Laie Bay and joined the festivities.

The Mormon missionary community experienced initial hardships in farming the barren land and, at times, they held on by faith alone. Once adequate water supplies were discovered, however, the harvests were abundant and the community grew and prospered.

The beautiful white temple that stands at Laie today was built of volcanic rock from Oahu's Koʻolau Mountains, and coral rock from the sea, both pulverized to a fine powder for concrete. This temple, the seventh Mormon temple in the world, was dedicated November 27, 1919.

In 1954, the President of The Church of Jesus Christ of Latter-day Saints, David O. McKay, announced the church's intention to found a college in Hawaiʻi. The following September, 1955, The Church College of Hawaiʻi at Laie welcomed its first 153 students.

Today the 200-acre school is the Hawaiʻi Campus of Brigham Young University in Utah, the largest private denominational school in the United States. It offers a first-class academic curriculum to students from around the world, many of whom could not otherwise afford higher education.

Working Together

The Polynesian Cultural Center has become an environment in which the young people live out the brotherhood embodied in both the Mormon faith and the Polynesian tradition.

Older, respected Polynesians from the various Pacific islands act as leaders and counselors to the students. Believing that the family is the heart of society, the elders form extended families with the students who have left their own relatives behind. They share with them an appreciation of their heritage and, as a result, the Polynesian villages at the Center are not only museums, they are living, vital links to home. They are crucibles of culture.

Helping Preserve Polynesian Heritage

In many areas of the Pacific, the Polynesian way of life has changed dramatically. Not only do the Polynesians often find themselves on the outskirts of the economic mainstream in their own homelands but their ancient culture is in danger of being entirely eclipsed by modern society. These changes have come within living memory of the older generations.

Men and women, the invaluable keepers of tradition, pass on their knowledge, arts, crafts and philosophy to the next generation. The students are nurtured on their heritage while acquiring the education they need for equality in modern society. The Center brings these elements together.

Work is play when it's work that's enjoyed. Obviously, these young people enjoy what they're doing. It's as if they give a party every

day (except Sunday, the "Sabbath") and the whole wide world comes. They climb tall coconut palms, break open the fruit and offer it. They teach the hula. They sing, play musical instruments, serve food and answer questions. They are stars and they shine brightly. Their enthusiasm is contagious. They are the primary reason everyone who comes to the Polynesian Cultural Center has such a grand time.

The story of Laie is the story of diverse cultures uniting to fulfill a prophetic dream. It is evidenced not only in the faces of Laie's generations but in the dedication celebrations and ceremonies of new chapels, a university, a temple and a living cultural center.

The hospitality of the Polynesians is known throughout the world and in Laie it is centered in the warmth and generosity shown towards the many guests who travel from near and far.

5

The Polynesians

The ancestors of the Polynesians bequeathed a love of the sea, a longing for voyaging, skills in creating native crafts, the joy of hospitality and the enthusiastic capacity for feasting.

W HEN EUROPEAN SAILORS FIRST VENTURED INTO THE PACIFIC, THEY WERE astonished to find a race of people who shared a common cultural heritage and similar languages living in isolated island groups scattered across an area larger than Europe and North America combined.

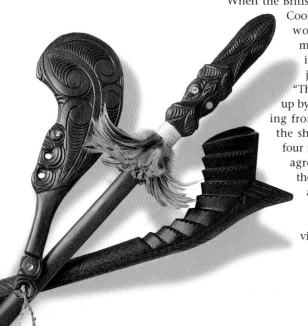

When the British explorer Captain James Cook first sighted Hawai'i, he wondered whether these most remote islands were inhabited and wrote in his journal of January 19, 1778, "This doubt was soon cleared up by seeing some canoes coming from off the shore towards the ships...There were three or four men in each and we were agreeably surprised to find them of the same nation as Otahiete (Tahiti) and the other islands we had visited." In his trav-els, Cook continued to note the similarities among these greatly separated island people.

The Greatest Story That's Never Been Told

The epic of the Polynesian exploration and colonization of the Pacific is the greatest story that's never been told.

Before the fall of Troy, while Europeans were still hugging their coastlines, afraid they might fall off the face of the flat earth, Polynesian sailors were discovering and charting the vast reaches of the Pacific.

Using sophisticated navigational skills employing the sun, moon and stars, the winds, sea birds and the ocean cur-rents, they set sail in huge voyaging canoes, 60 to 80 feet long. Their sails were plaited leaves, the ropes woven of coconut fiber and vines, their charts bits of shell and reed.

These brave men and women established new settlements wherever they went, bringing with them the plants and animals they would need for survival, and the cultural heritage they would pass to their children.

They carefully preserved all this knowledge, their genealogies, the deeds of their heroes and heroines, and their religion, in their chants and dances.

The world, however, did not easily accept the Polynesians' version of their history because it was not recorded in books. Lacking a written language and due to the ravages a tropical climate inflicts on material objects, there was no apparent evidence of these epic voyages of exploration. Westerners treated the stories as myth and claimed that the settlement of Polynesia was probably an accident, the result of rafts drifting in currents or fishermen blown to sea in a storm.

The Polynesian Pompeii

In 1981, on the island of Huahine in French Polynesia, archaeologists unearthed a 12-foot steering paddle, a 35-foot mast, huge bailers and planks from a canoe that measured 80 feet long.

Evidence indicated that a tidal wave had hit Huahine a thousand years ago, burying everything in the perfect mixture of sand and silt necessary to preserve the proof of the legends for future generations.

Where the Polynesians originally came from is still a matter of educated speculation. Current theories cite linguistic links to the languages of Southeast Asia. Other historians point to the voyages of Thor Heyerdahl's

Kon Tiki raft as evidence that the Polynesians first drifted from the Americas. A third group, using agricultural and blood type evidence, suggests that Polynesian roots could go back to both continents. No matter how these adventurers arrived, it is clear that they mastered the ocean. They made it their trade route and peopled a vast area of the Earth.

Following the Canoes Through History

Today, in the Carver's Hut at the Polynesian Cultural Center, skilled artisans using traditional tools, still carve outrigger canoes and fearsome *ki'i* or god images. Among the Center's most prized treasures are two priceless canoes–a 40-foot *camakau*, or Fijian canoe, and a Maori *waka taua*, an elaborately carved 60-foot canoe weighing two and a half tons.

The epic story of Polynesian canoes and migrations comes alive on the Center's giant IMAX® screen, 65 feet high and 89 feet wide. Viewers are drawn into the dawn of history as the dramatic production of "Polynesian Odyssey" unfolds. The cinematography is lavish, the drums, music and chants hypnotic and the story heroic.

The fascinating Migrations Museum documents the amazing history through its charts, displays and artifacts.

Every afternoon, lavishly decorated canoes sweep down canals becoming the stage where ancient legends are enacted in the colorful Pageant of the Long Canoes. There's music, dance, laughter and the honored tradition of story telling. In getting about the Center, visitors climb aboard canoes, discovering first one Polynesian village and then another, tracing the centuries-old path of oceanic migrations in less than half an hour. Indeed, the canoe is as much a part of the Polynesian Cultural Center experience as it was the focus of life in ancient Polynesia.

Voyaging canoes were decorated to endow special blessings of safety and purpose on the canoe itself and on its crew and travelers.

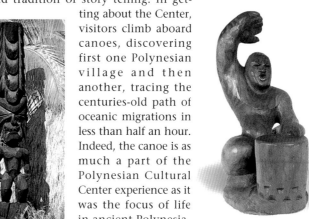

7

Discovering Polynesia in a Day

▲▲

Western Samoa

American Samoa

New Zealand

Fiji

Hawai'i

Marquesas

Tahiti

Tonga

THE DISTINCTIVE GATEWAY TO THE POLYNESIAN CULTURAL CENTER announces that this is a world apart from its surroundings, isolated, like the Pacific islands themselves. ◆ Students in flowing *muumuus* and exotic native costumes greet visitors, welcoming them as their ancestors did to the special world of Polynesia. The spirit of aloha they project is immediate, contagious and genuine. ◆ Stepping up to the box office windows, patrons learn that they are buying an experience—a day and a night in Polynesia, dinner and shows included. Like new arrivals in paradise, they are welcomed, swept up in the fun, and escorted to a day of activity. "This way to the villages of Polynesia."

Polynesians of the past took great pleasure in touring their own islands often going from village to village in large entourages. Visitors can see all seven Islands at the Polynesian Cultural Center as they glide by in double-hulled canoes.

· Samoa ·

Early explorers arrived in the Samoan islands about 1,000 B.C. From there, they set out on further voyages to Tahiti and the Marquesas. ◆ Fa'a Samoa, or the Samoan way of life, is still the dominant social force despite the pressures of modern civilization and the fact that the Samoan nation is divided. By treaty with the high chiefs in 1909, the Stars and Stripes was raised over the part of the island group that is now known as American Samoa. Neighboring Western Samoa is an independent nation. The two Samoas are intimately linked, with families straddling both sides of the international boundary. ◆ In both Samoas, the *matai*, or chief system, is the working social order. With the extended family as its nucleus, it is a pyramidal structure

Western samoa has a population of about 160,000 natives. American Samoa has approximately 44,600 people in 57 villages. The Samoan archipelago lies approximately between Hawai'i and New Zealand.

with the village chief administering affairs and making decisions. The family or village chief is responsible to the high chiefs, high talking chiefs and paramount chiefs—more than 20,000 chiefs in all. It is a system of behavior that has functioned well for over a thousand years. ◆ Christianity has been fervently embraced by the

Samoans. Prayers are said before every meal and most villages observe a communal prayer time at least once a day. There are more churches per capita than anywhere else in the world. According to a recent Fodor's Guide, "...at least one modern mission, American in origin, gives incomparably more than it receives, tithe-based though it is. That is the Mormon mission." The church has been the agent binding traditional Samoan values of caring with modern social concerns. ◆ Many Samoan people live on their verdant, volcanic islands, much as they have for centuries, in open-sided, thatch-roofed *fale*, or oval homes. They have an instinctive joy in life and are often called the Irish of the Pacific.

TALOFA~
Welcome to the Village of Samoa

No one can climb a coconut tree faster than a Samoan. With exuberant shouts, great wit and the energy of the very young, a Samoan, dressed in *lavalava*, scales a 40-foot tree as if it were a sandbox toy. He enjoys the cheers and applause as he poses among the tree-top coconuts for photographers.

Although no one these days needs to know how to start a fire with two sticks of wood, the Samoans, joking the whole time, show visitors how it is done, quickly. People continue to be absolutely fascinated by one of man's most basic and revolutionary discoveries. Obviously, it is the presentation, rather than what is presented, that draws and holds the crowds.

Fun is foremost at the Samoan village from the guest house to the *Maota Tofa*, the chief's house.

Visitors who begin their tour of the Polynesian Cultural Center in Samoa, may learn to weave for themselves a coconut frond sun visor. They will also learn to husk and crack a coconut and to tell the difference between coconut juice and coconut milk. Sampling the delicious nectars is part of the experience.

In the chief's house, there is a lecture, and a special opportunity to share in this gentle culture which has so much to teach the world.

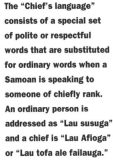

The "Chief's language" consists of a special set of polite or respectful words that are substituted for ordinary words when a Samoan is speaking to someone of chiefly rank. An ordinary person is addressed as "Lau susuga" and a chief is "Lau Afioga" or "Lau tofa ale failauga."

Every village in Samoa has a *malae* or village green where special ceremonies and activities are held, such as the traditional *ava* ceremony, Samoa's highest form of welcoming to extend hospitality and respect to visiting families, friends and important guests. Villagers ensure that the *malae* is landscaped as a showplace of welcome and pride.

The coconut tree has always had great significance in Samoan culture. Among the host names for the tree are "The Prince of Palms," "The Mother Tree," and "The Tree of Life."

· Aotearoa ·

The first people to arrive at the islands now known as New Zealand were Polynesians who sailed from their ancestral homeland which they called Hawaiki and whose actual location has been lost in time. The first expedition, about 950 A.D., was led by a chief, Kupe, who returned home with precise navigational instructions for reaching the new land, Aotearoa. About 1150 there was another voyage and, finally, in 1350, seven canoes of colonists arrived. Today the Maori people trace their ancestry to the canoes named Tainui, Te Arawa, Aotea, Tokomaru, Takitimu, Mataatua and Kurahaupo. ◆ Recent archaeological evidence suggests that the Maori found a group of people, the Moriori, also Polynesians, already dwelling in Aotearoa.

No one has any idea where they came from, but they were superseded by the more aggressive Maori. ◆ The new home had all the familiar elements of the tropical islands the Maori had left behind, plus alpine mountains, fjords, glaciers, lakes, swift rivers and vast forests. The climate ranged from sub-tropical to temperate. ◆ Adapting to the new conditions, the Maori built homes of timber, became the most skilled woodworkers in Polynesia, and made their clothing of woven flax rather than tree bark. ◆ They developed a tribal society ruled by hereditary chiefs and a powerful priesthood. The tribes became rivals and lived in fortified villages, *pa*, centered around a *marae*, or main courtyard. ◆ Ceremony was, and remains, important to Maori culture and nobody entered a village without elaborate ritual. They developed great oratorical skills and poetic use of language. ◆ New Zealand was discovered by the Dutch

According to Maori myth, a chief named Mataroa was the first man ever tattooed on earth. The craft is considered highly sacred to the Maoris who apply it uniquely by cutting grooves into the skin. ■ The carved figures on the walls of Maori meeting houses represent the ancestral history of the tribe. ■ Poi balls were used by Maori women for telling stories and imitating natural sounds and motions in their dances.

explorer Able Tasman. Europeans came in droves to exploit the natural resources. In 1840, the British signed The Treaty of Waitangi with the Maori chiefs, promising to protect their lands from exploitation and making New Zealand a British colony. ◆ Maoris today comprise about 12 percent of the predominantly European population of New Zealand.

KIA ORA ~ *Welcome to the Village of Aotearoa*

At the magnificently carved entrance to the Maori stockade, a "warrior" approaches, brandishing his *taiaha* lance, posturing and grimacing menacingly. He places a carving or sprig of greenery at the visitors' feet. If no one retrieves the offering, it means war. If a visitor picks up the sprig, it signifies he comes in peace. He is welcomed and the visit begins.

In one corner of the village, visitors are asked to join in stick games, requiring concentration, coordination and a sense of humor. On the other side of the *marae*, a beautiful young Maori student teaches poi ball twirling, the unique skill that accompanies so many Maori dances. Outside the *Whare Puni*, or family dwelling, women weave the unusual red, white and black Maori patterns worn by men and women in their clothing. There are lectures on the importance of these patterns and the weav-

ing techniques used to achieve them. There are also lectures on history and the Maori art of tattooing.

Proud of ancient victories, the Maori share their knowledge of weaponry. In a hut beside the lagoon is the carvers' workshop where artisans sculpt and shape wood in the manner of their ancestors. A little farther away is a great war canoe, built to carry 40 warriors to sea—in style. The canoe is not only a maritime marvel, but a work of art.

One of the most stirring experiences of the Maori village is the ceremonial blowing of the *pukaea*, a long slender horn reminiscent of those blown from the towers of ancient European castles.

At the Polynesian Cultural Center, New Zealanders study the honored traditions and learn the fine arts and crafts of the first settlers of their beautiful Land of the Long White Cloud.

· Fiji ·

Fiji is a nation of 322 islands spread like a horseshoe in the blue Pacific embracing the Koro Sea. ◆ The early Fijians were the pottery makers of Polynesia. Archaeologists, dating shards of their Lapita pottery, estimate the ancestors of the Polynesians were settled in Fiji near 1500 B.C. They were skilled seafarers, builders and weavers of sennet and palm fronds. ◆ European rediscovery took place island by island, over a period of 300 years beginning in 1643. Captain William Bligh, after the famous mutiny, rowed through the treacherous reef-strewn Fijian waters, recording in his journal all that he observed. ◆ Fiji's sandalwood forests attracted foreign traders who were followed by Christian missionaries. ◆ To stabilize conditions in their rapidly changing society, the Fijians, under High Chief Cakobau, voluntarily ceded their islands to Great Britain in 1874. British rule continued until independence in 1970. ◆ During the colonial period, the English established cotton and sugar plantations. Finding the Fijians uninterested in their monetary economy, the English imported workers from India. Today, people of Indian descent outnumber native Fijians by a small margin, although almost all the land is still controlled by Fijians. Both peoples traditionally practice the unusual rite of fire-walking. The Fijians believe that a legendary spirit god gave the gift to the Sawau tribesmen who live on Beqa Island. When Sawau people walk across the white hot stones, they are acting out their history. Indians of the Madras sect of the Hindu faith

Fiji is at the crossroads between Melanesia and Polynesia and the traditions from both areas are evidenced throughout the archipelago.

19

practice fire-walking as a form of penance.

◆ Though outnumbered in their homeland, Fijians, with the encouragement of their elders, and through the young people educated at the Polynesian Cultural Center, are saving their arts and beautiful *meke* (song-dances) for posterity.

BULA VINAKA~
Welcome to the Village of Fiji

The tall graceful thatched roof of the Fijian *Bure Kalou*, stands dramatically against the skyline, making the Fijian village the easiest to spot in the Center. People are drawn toward it, crossing one of the bridges leading into the village. There they are greeted by a fierce-looking but friendly Fijian "warrior." They are invited into the Fijian dwellings, their meeting house, their place of work and even their unique retirement home. The house of the chief is distinguished by the cowry shells on the roof.

Every afternoon, the Fijian students stage a fashion show, parading the fascinating traditional dress of both men and women of the nobility, the warrior class and common people.

Beside the lagoon, a rope maker practices his ancient craft, weaving from the tough fiber of the coconut, the same type of ropes that held the sails, caught the fish, and lashed the canoes and homes of his ancestors. At the Polynesian Cultural Center, master rope makers from Fiji, continue to teach the young people the honored techniques that might be lost due to the introduction of synthetic fibers.

The Fijians also teach visitors their form of lei making with dried material tinted with natural dyes. There are demonstrations of copra making, again using the bountiful coconut, plus historical lectures, hauntingly beautiful bamboo music, and Fijian dance lessons. Here, you will find a total sharing of the customs and traditions brought from that sprinkling of reef-hugged islands.

The major art forms of the Fijians include the extensive use of *voivoi*, or pandanus leaves in home crafts and dance paraphernalia and the sculpting of clay into distinctive pottery.

"Bula Vinaka," the Fijian greeting means more than "hello." It also conveys "Good health be with you always." ■ Fijians used the *derua* or bamboo instruments to provide the rhythms to accompany music and dance. The bamboo length is held in the hand with the closed end down and when struck on the ground, resonates. The shorter the bamboo, the higher the sound and visa-versa.

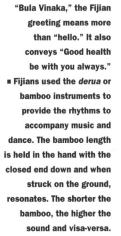

◆ Hawai'i ◆

The story of Hawai'i is typical of what happened in most of Polynesia. The details differ, but as with other Polynesian cultures, there is more similarity than diversity. ◆ Living for centuries in isolation, the Hawaiians developed a unique culture, in harmony with their limited island environment, ordered a highly structured society of nobility and commoners, and used their religion as a system of law. They cared for their ill with an amazing pharmacoepia of natural ingredients and spiritual self-help, recorded their history in complicated and lyrical

chants and dances, and prized both their artists and their artistic expressions in woodwork, tapa (bark cloth) and featherwork. ◆ The impact of the encounter with the rest of the world was immediate and devastating. Within a few years, foreign diseases, to which the Hawaiians had developed no immunities, decimated the population. New plants and animals altered the environment, and their traditional culture was virtually eclipsed. ◆ Thanks to both the steadfastness of people who quietly nurtured aspects of their heritage, and efforts such as that of the Polynesian Cultural Center, there

is currently a strong renaissance of Hawaiian culture through-out the Islands. Young people studying their past develop pride in their heritage and face the future with confidence.

The *hula* in Hawaiian culture instructs, inspires and entertains. The dances are performed by both men and women with themes historically important to Hawaiians. The appeal in *hula* lies in the graceful movements, the easily identifiable costumes, the accessories crafted from nature and the music accompaniments.

23

At the Polynesian Cultural Center, the Hawaiians enjoy their *kauhale* or many dwellings, used as they were anciently by an extended family unit or *ohana*. Each building represents a specific use: sleeping, eating, working, arts training, etc.

ALOHA~

Welcome to the Hawaiian Village

Fishnets hang drying in the sun beside the lagoon. A waterfall cascades through lush greenery bright with flowers. A carved *ki'i* or god image presides over the village, as in ancient times.

Central to the Hawaiian village is the *lo'i kalo*, a flooded field of taro. *Taro* is the Hawaiian staff of life, the brother of mankind. The cooked leaves taste like spinach. The corm is pounded for *poi* or baked like a potato in the *imu*, underground oven. These days it is also made into *taro* chips, similar to potato chips. So essential is this beautiful crop, it has come to symbolize the enduring Hawaiian culture. *Poi* is pounded at the village's *halau*, or house of learning, and shared with anyone brave enough to try the notorious purple paste. Baked *taro* is also served.

Hawaiians drew their sustenance from both land and sea. The dramatic technique of throw-net fishing is demonstrated.

Fascinating lectures reveal little known aspects of Hawaii's history, from early settlement through the monarchy era. The *Hale Ali'i* or chief's house dominates the rest of the *kauhale*.

A Hawaiian family dwelled in many houses rather than just one. The village has a *Hale Noho*, the main family dwelling, and a *Hale Mua*, the men's eating house. In ancient times, if the head of the household was a fisherman, there would be a Hale *Wa'a*, a canoe shed, such as the one by the village shore, and a *Hale Hoahu*, or shed where he kept his nets and the implements of his trade.

The Hawaiian Village also has a *Hale Ulana*, or weaving hut, where craftsmen perpetuate the art of *lauhala* work, making intricate baskets, fans and toys. Visitors are invited to participate.

The eerie, commanding sound of the conch shell horn blowing across the village announces the arrival of royalty, and signals the start of important ceremonies.

The most famous aspect of Hawaiian culture is the *hula*, known throughout the world for its graceful movements. "Keep your eyes on the hands," a popular island song goes, and learn Hawaii's story. At the *Halau Hula*, students continue the tradition, sharing the history of the dance in words and motions. In the shade of a spreading *hau* tree, visitors are taught basic *hula*. The *'auana* or modern form is danced to guitar and ukulele, the string instrument introduced by early Portuguese settlers in Hawai'i. The powerful *hula kahiko* is accompanied by traditional *hula* drums which are fashioned from gourds, wood and sharkskin.

Anciently, the art of *hula* was very sacred. Therefore, *hula* implements were stored in special houses built on temple compounds.

■ *Poi* is a highly nutritious paste made from the *taro* root. It is usually used as a staple food to accompany meat and fish.

In ancient Hawai'i, canoes were hollowed out of straight tree trunks, smoothed with pumice stones and water-proofed with *kukui* nut oil.

25

· Marquesas ·

Wild and lonely islands with names like Nuku Hiva, Ua Huka and Hiva Oa are besieged by the ocean and whipped by the wind. Of these 10 islands, only six are inhabited. ◆ The ancient valley people of the Marquesas, separated from each other by mountainous terrain and treacherous seas, developed insular little societies, jealous and warlike. Their artwork, particularly in wood, was striking and they

left behind beautiful bowls, fan handles, intricate ironwood war clubs and impressive *tikis*. They also carved massive god images in stone. ◆ It was from these islands that expeditions set forth to colonize Hawai'i to the North and Easter Island to the East. ◆ The islands were discovered by the Spanish in 1595 and named Las Marquesas de Mendoza. Drawing near the coast, the

The twelve islands of Marquesas are still considered to be exotic and mysterious by outsiders. The Marquesans are noted for their native handicrafts, especially their distinctive styles of wood carving.

ship San Jerónimo was approached by a fleet of outrigger canoes crewed by 400 men whom the Spanish described as robust, light-skinned with blue tattoos, and wearing their hair long and loose. ◆ Contact was the beginning of the end for the Marquesan people. Foreign diseases, slave raids, the introduction of opium, the continuation of their

own warfare and cannibalism killed 95 percent of the population. ◆ The Marquesas Islands are today a part of French Polynesia. Significant archaeological sites at Hane on Ua Huka have shed much light on the mysteries of early Polynesian migrations. Norwegian explorer and anthropologist Thor Heyerdahl lived on Fatu Hiva in 1936 and wrote a book, "Aku Aku", about his time in this remote place.

Marquesan tattoos were intricately engraved in the skin using a bone needle tipped with indelible plant-dye. Young men were tattooed between the ages of 15 and 20, girls between the ages 7 and 12, in separate tattoo houses.

28

The "tohua" is the hereditary property of a given chief and is part of his family's residential complex. Here, important ceremonies were performed and celebratory feasts were conducted. ■ The ideal for Marquesan beauty required narrow faces with sloping foreheads and flattened noses which were molded by pressure massage during infancy.

KAOHA ~ *Welcome to the Village of the Marquesas*

What was lost is found. The students at the Center have helped in preserving the Marquesan culture by studying early records and interviewing elders about the old way of life.

The Marquesan Village at the Polynesian Cultural Center, once just an exhibit, is now a living, vital place. Actually a ceremonial compound, or *tohua*, it vibrates with the spirit that once made the Marquesas the dispersal point for Polynesian migration.

Visitors relax in the shade of the impressive coral block structures while the *Haka Puaka*, the lusty pig hunting dance, bursts from the dawn of time. To the beat of ancient drums, men in feathers and red loin cloths portray the courage and cunning of the hunt, never turning their backs on the *Ha'e Haka'iki*, the chief's house.

Tattoo is actually a Polynesian word. Body patterns were designed to confer prestige, power and protection. Only the firstborn child, male or female, was tattooed. From their ranks, chiefs were chosen. Today, anyone can tap into the prestige at the Marquesan Village and be painted with a (non-permanent) traditional tattoo.

The Marquesan village also serves as nature's own first aid station. Extensive research has been done into early Polynesian pharmacology. Medical practices were quite sophisticated, and doctors treated the patient holistically, healing both body and spirit. The most popular medication on village shelves today is the aloe sunburn remedy.

Samples of breadfruit, *taro* or surprisingly good boiled green bananas are free fuel for continuing the day's tour of the Polynesian Cultural Center.

Buildings in the Marquesan compound are constructed of Hawaiian coral rather than the basalt rock the Marquesans used in their homeland. The decision to use coral is one the practical Polynesians would have made, for they were adept at using locally available material.

Through lectures and story-telling, the history of the little-known Marquesas Islands is shared. The most often asked question is, "Where are these islands?" A map at the village entrance pinpoints their location in the Pacific, as part of the great Polynesian Triangle.

· Tahiti ·

Tahiti is the name of one island in the Society Islands, a group which is part of the vast territory of French Polynesia. Today, Tahiti serves as the territorial capital of French Polynesia which includes the Society Islands–Moorea, Bora Bora, Raiatea and Huahine as well as the Tuamotu Archipelago, Austral Islands Gambier Archipelago and Marquesan Islands. ◆ Current migration theories place the settlement of Tahiti at 300 A.D. when Samoans established the first colonies in the verdant, dramatically beautiful islands. Two centuries later, canoes from Tahiti set out for Hawai'i and Easter Island, and around 1000 A.D. they colonized the Cook Islands and New Zealand. ◆ The Tahitians were ruled by a priestly class headquartered on Raiatea. In 1767, the British ship Dolphin sailed into the harbor of Tahiti and hoisted the Union Jack. A year later, the French Captain Bougainville came and claimed the islands for France. With the assistance of European firearms, the Tahitian chiefs of the Pomare clan established their supremacy and ruled until 1880 when King Pomare V signed away his kingdom to France in return for a comfortable pension.

Golden-skinned Tahitian women still wear bright pareaus with fragrant flowers behind their ears and handsome Tahitian men still fish on the reef at night and play their guitars and wooden drums.

The cession followed decades of political pressure from both France and England. ◆ The prehistory of Tahiti is just beginning to be explored. Vast populations lived in the forested mountains. Mysteriously, the people departed their high fortresses, leaving behind foundations of homes, temples and agricultural terraces to be hidden by the jungle. Today these settlements are being mapped and researched. Ancient artifacts linking Tahiti with other islands of Polynesia are being examined and categorized. The task is complicated by the fact that nuclear testing in the

Pacific has invalidated the radio carbon dating techniques, commonly used to determine antiquity. ◆ The islands of Tahiti range from low coral atolls to the rugged grandeur of Maupiti's sea cliffs and towering green Mount Orohena on Tahiti. Misty waterfalls, bright flowers and turquoise lagoons complete the pictures that French painter Paul Gauguin immortalized in art. ◆ The Polynesians of Tahiti speak both French and Tahitian, and, with the growth of tourism, many also speak English. Thousands of miles away, Tahitian culture is being rediscovered by visitors to the Polynesian Cultural Center.

IA ORA NA ~ *Welcome to the Village of Tahiti*

The wooden drums of Tahiti pound out across the Center, calling, intriguing, as the islands themselves have always done.

Visitors are swept up in the movement, the energy and color of the Tahitian Village. They are dressed in dancing skirts, invited to the *Tahua Orira'a* (dance platform) and taught the exciting Tahitian version of the *hula*, the one that rocks the palm trees. They are encouraged to match the boldness of the Tahitians. Everyone joins in. There isn't an idle bystander, not when the air is charged with such excitement.

A plantation at the Tahitian Village grows bananas, sweet potato, pineapple, and that staple of Tahitian cuisine, breadfruit. At the *Fare Tutu*, there is a demonstration of Tahitian cooking and visitors are offered food cooked in an earth oven.

At the *Fare Ravera'a Ohipa*, women fashion skirts from hibiscus bark, while the men at the *Fare Tautai* mend fishing nets and make marvelous and highly decorative fishing traps. Tahitian crafts, especially beautiful sea shell work, are exhibited at the *Fare Pote'e*.

Intricate Tahitian shellwork is used to adorn dancing costumes, home furnishings, hats, baskets, and many other artifacts.
■ The traditional dances of Tahiti are still performed with skill and enthusiasm. Lively competitions take place in Papeete with dance troupes from throughout French Polynesia.

The women of Tahiti are still taught the traditional skills of their ancestors. They weave pandanus baskets, string intricate shell *leis*, chant old songs, decorate dancing skirts, braid flower head wreaths and prepare earthoven meals.

· Tonga ·

Tapa cloth is made from the inner bark of the paper mulberry tree. Every day (except Sundays) the sound of women rhythmically beating *tapa* is heard throughout Tonga. Today, *tapa* is marketed primarily for ceremonial occasions such as the traditional gift-giving at weddings and funerals.

Tonga is one of the few countries in the world, and the only one in Polynesia, never to be colonized by a European power. Its royal family, now headed by His Majesty King Taufa'ahau Tupou IV, has been ruling continuously for over a thousand years. ◆ According to Tongan legend, the demigod Maui, who appears in most Polynesian mythology and for whom the Hawaiian island of Maui is named, fished up the Tongan island from the ocean floor with a Samoan fishhook. ◆ The warriors of Tonga were feared throughout Polynesia and their *kalia*, or canoes, carried their armies to far shores. At one time the empire of the Tu'i Tonga, or hereditary king, extended from Rotuma in the west to Niue in the east, and included much of Samoa. ◆ Today the

country is a constitutional monarchy with a parliament. Their laws are based on Christian values with a strict observance of the sabbath that will remind American visitors of quiet Sundays decades ago in their small towns. The present king is the son of the beloved Queen Salote who won the hearts of the world when, in a magnificent and typically Tongan gesture of respect, she

rode to the coronation of Queen Elizabeth II of England in an open carriage in torrential rain. ◆ Tongan arts are still beautifully handcrafted without mass production. Their *tapa* cloth, mainly from the island of Tongatapu, is especially notable. All natural dyes are used

to achieve the intricate geometric patterns. For both ceremonial and everyday clothing, men and women still wear the *ta'ovala*, a mat made of finely woven pandanus leaves and tied as a skirt. The best mats are passed from generation to generation as prized

heirlooms. ◆ The islands of Tonga are mainly low-lying atolls with still active volcanoes. The largest building in the island group is the Mormon temple on Tongatapu.

MALO E LELEI~
Welcome to the Village of Tonga

The neat, thatched buildings of the Tongan Village are distinguished by their magnificent *tapa*. These huge sheets of layered cloth, made from the bark of the paper mulberry plant, are among the finest examples of this typical Polynesian art.

Tongan students, schooled by their elders at the Polynesian Cultural Center in the ways of the centuries-old craft, proudly show visitors how soft, lovely garments are made.

Because Tongans are extremely proud of their royal family, their village would not be complete without a reminder of nobility. Dominating the complex is a replica of the late Queen Salote's summer home. There is also a *Fale Mohe*, a sleeping house; a *Fale Kautaha*, women's workshop; and the *Fale Fakataha*, or village meeting house where matters of behavior and discipline are discussed and decided.

Under the spreading tree canopy of the village, students share the graceful and energetic dances of their homeland.

A village highlight is the *tā nafa*, an exuberant, hilarious drum program involving very large drums, larger drummers and visitor participation.

Visitors are also challenged to try the seemingly simple game of *lafo*, akin to shuffleboard, and they are taught to weave toys and souvenir headbands from coconut leaves.

The Tongan village is responsible for cooking the pigs for the Polynesian Cultural Center's nightly *luau*. With great ceremony, the roasted pigs are lifted from their *'umu* or underground oven and paraded to the *luau* buffet.

The Tongan Village is a place to savor Polynesia with those who know the culture best, because even today, the fiercely independent Tongans still revere and live their heritage.

36

The men of Polynesia pride themselves not only in their entertainment skills, but also in their abilities in oratory, navigation, housebuilding, fishing, etc. Cooking their families' daily food in earthovens is traditionally rewarding for them. The Polynesian Cultural Center's *luau* pig is cooked by the young men of Tonga every day.

The Pageant of the Long Canoes

▲▲

"Ancient Legends of Polynesia" Across the lagoons they glide, the long, beautifully decorated double-hulled canoes of Polynesia. They carry kings, queens, chiefs, even gods. They pass the villages along the shore. They sail under bridges, continuing under a canopy of waving palm trees. The brightly costumed passengers and the visitors lining the shore will soon share a revered tradition of Polynesia: the art of telling stories through chants, music and dance, and they will do it in the context of the canoe, the lifeline linking far flung islands and peoples. In Hawai'i, the story-telling medium is *hula*, for the Tahitians it's *aparima*, the Fijians call it *meke*. The names differ, but the legends are loved by all people of the Pacific. ◆ In the absence of a written language, the Polynesians danced their way through time, committing their history, genealogies, and epic adventures of gods and kings to memory and music. The tales illustrate the messages and values necessary for the survival of the next generation.

The oral traditions of the Polynesians preserve their history, passed from storyteller to storyteller, imbuing each telling with the luster of traditional words, phrases and gestures.

The canoes burst upon the scene, heralded by music. The Hawaiian canoe bears a rainbow as the dancers relate the story of the Goddess of the Feathery Rain and the chief who fell in love with her but didn't know her name, so he was rejected. It was his grandmother who helped him win the love of the Rainbow Princess.

Always dramatic, the Fijians tell the origins of their amazing ability to walk on fire. The power was given to them by the half-eel, half-human demigod Tui Namoliwai, the leader of a band of elves. To this day, some Fijians can walk unharmed across superheated rocks in a rite they call *vilavilairevo*, always protected by thousands of elves.

The Polynesians performers delight not only in the cultural dances of their home island but in the traditions of fellow Polynesians.

"The Pageant of the Long Canoes" is a reminder of the fleets of ancient voyaging canoes carrying Polynesians who were strong in the courage of discovery and in the celebration of life.

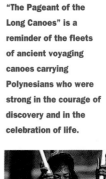

The lagoon stage unifies the islands of Polynesia, all of the same origin but distinct in their differences and their similarities.

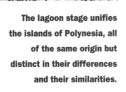

There's an eel god aboard the Samoan story canoe, too. He falls in love with Sina, a maiden who lives beside a stream. Her parents don't like the looks of this slippery suitor and kill him. Before he dies, he asks Sina to bury his head by the stream. He promises her a special tree will grow to symbolize the happy times they shared. The tree was the coconut palm, the Pacific tree of life. In husking the fruit, Sina discovered each nut bore the two eyes and the mouth of her eel friend, Tuna.

The Maori canoe of Aotearoa vividly illustrates a tale of love and war as the young chief Ponga woos and wins Puhihuia, a maiden from a rival village. When her avenging clansmen try to bring her home, Ponga bravely defends her. A wedding takes place aboard the Maori canoes.

The divine origins of the royal family of Tonga are the theme of that country's robust canoe pageant. After dance battles with celestial beings, Tangaloa, the god of the sky, resurrects his murdered son, Ahoeitu, and sends him back to Earth as the first Tu'i Tonga, or crowned king of Tonga. He endows him with divine powers and great wisdom. His descendants still rule Tonga, the only remaining kingdom in Polynesia.

Tahiti's wildly costumed legend is about Raka, a brave chief who sets out on a quest to find his parents, who had been captured by the giant bird Matuku when he was an infant. Armed with a magical spear, he sets sail aboard an enchanted canoe. After conquering monstrous sea creatures, he kills Matuku himself. Raka's warriors pluck the giant bird and use the feathers to camouflage their canoe. Now cleverly disguised, they are able to penetrate Matuku's island fortress and rescue Raka's parents. The celebration honoring the parents and the faithful son rocks the lagoon.

With all the fun, the noise, clowning, laughter, and music in the colorful Pageant of the Long Canoes, lessons in love, duty, faith and honor are easily absorbed and embraced. When the last canoe glides away, it leaves in its wake great happiness, a longing to know more—and a need for more film.

The foremost hero of Polynesian legends is the demigod Maui with islands, landmarks, structures, canoes and tools all named in his honor.

The Grand Finale of a Day in Polynesia

▲▲

The Spirit of the Islands in Our Spectacular Evening Revue A dramatic procession of torches opens the largest Polynesian revue in the world. Ninety sizzling minutes later the power-packed musical ends in the blaze of a grand finale backed by towering volcanic fires. In between is a dazzling display of music and dances from all of Polynesia. It is undoubtedly the best show in the entire Pacific. The cast numbers more than a hundred; the music is spellbinding, the costuming, lighting and timing are thoroughly professional and exceptionally beautiful.

The dancers of Hawai'i introduce with ancient *kahiko* dances, *hula 'auana* and elegant solos, celebrating the beauty of Hawaii's mountains and windward Oahu. The Hawaiian culture has remained a vital force even with the vast changes that have enveloped the islands, because young people like those on the stage of the Polynesian Cultural Center cultivate the ancient spirit of *mana*.

Polynesian culture means music and dance. These expressions are an integral part of Polynesian folklore and lifestyle. They are their artistic translations of traditional words and thought put to meaningful movement.

From behind a fountaining curtain of water, a Fijian chief costumed in voluminous precious *masi* bark cloth strides forward to lead his people, the warrior dancers. *Lali* drums beat as the chief delivers his *Ni Sa Bula*, welcome. Included is a spear-jabbing Fijian war chant which moves to a wild victory dance and is softened by the fan dance of the women offering thanks for the safe return of the men. With colorful costuming and intricate steps, the men enact a battle of the legendary dwarf warriors from the mystic

With every performance, the beauty, dignity, grace and joy of the Polynesians is reaffirmed in the most spectacular evening revue in Hawai'i.

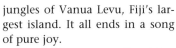

jungles of Vanua Levu, Fiji's largest island. It all ends in a song of pure joy.

To the Samoans, cultural traditions are highly significant in their daily lives, like fire dancing, family ceremonies and feasting. Maidens enact the traditional *kava*-drinking ceremony, releasing energetic fun. The lovely daughter of the high chief, in a dress sewn from hundreds of glossy leaves and a crown of feathers and human hair dances with exceptional grace. It is the fire dancers, however, who steal the show every time. The warm-up act is a trio of red hot clowns who literally play with fire, sitting on it, falling into it, burning their grass skirts. The crowd roars. When a champion fire knife dancer charges on stage, almost torching the front-row audience, everyone is primed. In greeting, he holds out his burning hand. No one will shake it. He laughs and whirls into his fiery act, his torch lit on both ends. He's an inspired artist, twirling, stomping, eating flames, pushing himself to new limits every night. From the smoky shadows, a legion of fire dancers join him in a spirited conflagration.

In contrast, the Tongans share their love of the sacred in an enchanting sitting dance spurred by throbbing drums. The *'akau ta nafa*

Music and dance in Polynesia reflect a deep joy of life and love of heritage.

Performances in the home and in public are encouraged in Polynesia and are considered a gift to be shared and admired.

drumsticks of the chief drummer, with their long white streamers, seem to fly from drum to drum, pushing emotions to the edge. In celebrating the *Lakalaka*, the Tongans honor the Christian traditions of Tonga where law still forbids all but essential businesses from opening on Sunday.

The Maori pick up the spiritual thread, believing that the greatest spirit of mana is earned by serving others. Their lyrical songs and dances portray the journeys and heroics of the demigod Maui, legendary patron of all Polynesia. In their breathtaking fire poi segment, the women thank Maui for the gift of fire. *Taku Mana*, the closing dance, depicts Maui's struggle with *Hine Nui te Po* when he fails to conquer death. His grandfather reminds him, "one must die to rise again."

At that telling moment, the Tahitians sweep onto the stage, full of life and fun. Wildly energetic happiness is their special spirit. The women try to outdo each other in

the velocity of their hip swinging. The men bring their brawn to the act. The costumes are lavish with traditional high headdresses and gyrating grass skirts. Without even an ember displayed, the Tahitian dances are incendiary, pulsating with vitality.

The entire cast fills the stage for the finale, "Bula Laie", written by the late Fijian composer Isireli Racule and popularized in English by Elvis Presley as "Drums of the Islands." One hundred strong they sing while waterfalls cascade down the stage cliffs and volcanoes erupt in crimson flames. They're all here, the fierce and the beautiful, in the prime of their lives, giving their best to the people who have journeyed from all points of the compass to meet them at the Polynesian Cultural Center, the gathering place of the Pacific.

These bright young people in their native dress are the hope of their homelands. They have learned well the traditions of their ancestors, and will return with the skills and leadership ability to propel their countries into the future with confidence, integrity, and pride in who they are and in the heritage they carry. More than 30,000 students have danced their way through college. More than 25 million people have made it possible by coming to meet them and learn their ways at the Polynesian Cultural Center. That's the spirit of the Islands!

The vitality of Polynesian drum rhythms invites both performers and audience members to move to its beat and pulse.

Fire has become a staple feature in Polynesian performances as demonstrated in the Samoan fire dances and the Maori flaming poi ball twirling.

The art of quilt making was learned from 19th Century European and American missionaries. This beautiful practice is still preserved not only in Hawai'i where it has become an important tradition, but in other Polynesian islands as well.

Using a variety of plants, Polynesian women have been able to create highly useful and decorative items—hats, skirts, cloaks, leis, mats, baskets and other home accessories.

Experience the Polynesian Cultural Center

▲▲

C ANOES GLIDE ALONG THE CANALS AND LAGOONS PAST THE SHORELINES OF TAHITI, Tonga, Hawai'i, Samoa, Aotearoa (New Zealand) and the mysterious Marquesas. Well marked paths meander through the villages, past riots of tropical vegetation, swaying palms and sleepy lagoons. There are maps, signs and best of all, friendly student guides to point the way, answer questions, make suggestions and hint at their favorite options—which are probably activities of their own home village.

The sound most commonly heard is laughter. The students enjoy what they are doing. They are witty with the brightness and enthusiasm of youth. They have everyone learning the *hula*, tasting *poi*, weaving palm leaves. They entice guests into a Tongan house, where they have their pictures taken with a tall, handsome chief. But always, there's the beat of a drum around the bend, something else happening. Like the Polynesian voyagers of old, visitors are drawn eagerly onward to the next adventure.

It may be the arrival of beautifully decorated canoes bearing colorfully costumed warriors, lovely goddesses, hapless maidens, brave rescuers, stern kings and smiling queens all decked out for the Pageant of the Long Canoes. This 30-minute photogenic water show gives vibrant new life to the old tales of Polynesia.

The Polynesian Cultural Center has become an active site for extraordinary cultural exchanges. Special events often highlight visiting cultural performing groups such as Aborigines from Australia, Marquesans and Tahitians from French Polynesia, fire walkers from Fiji, etc.

Refreshment stands made of carved canoes dispense ice cream and frosty guava and coconut drinks. They are conveniently, temptingly situated throughout the Center.

Shoppers will discover unique treasures, usually not available beyond the borders of Polynesia at the new "Treasures of Polynesia" shopping plaza. Baskets, decorative fish traps, authentic hula skirts, woodcarvings and handwoven items are among the offerings. There is a special section for the best crafts and exports of each island group. The artwork of

noted Island artists is honored and available. There will be handblown glass guaranteed for a lifetime, master woodworks, plus original canvases as well as lithographs and inexpensive posters of beautiful Pacific scenes.

The Museum Store is headquarters for video tapes of the Center's major productions, including "Mana!"—the complete evening show—and "Portrait of Polynesia," an excellent overall visual souvenir of the Center. By calling the store's toll free number (1-800-283-3108) visitors may order these and other professional video presentations of the Center that will bring back all the magic of a day in Polynesia.

The Yoshimura Store is a typical plantation store specializing in island treats. For generations, Hawaiian children have loved "shave ice," the tropical version of the snow cone. There are also snack bars and other stands for such refreshments as macadamia nut ice cream in a pineapple boat, pink guava sherbet, sliced iced pineapple, cold fresh coconut and familiar favorites such as hot dogs and hamburgers.

Right in the heart of the Polynesian Cultural Center is the Missionary Complex, a tribute to the selfless dedication of the early Christian missionaries in the South Pacific. Built in the 1850s style, which incorporated elements of both American and traditional Polynesian architectural design, the missionary home is a snug shelter hung with magnificent Hawaiian quilts.

Every guest at the Polynesian Cultural Center has a myriad of choices from among the unique cultural experiences of Polynesia. Wherever they come from, they will leave with special encounters and momentos which they will cherish for a lifetime.

Experience ⟨THE⟩ Polynesian Cultural Center

▲▲

At the Close of Day

When the sun goes down the pace picks up at the Polynesian Cultural Center. Many people return to their favorite village for the colorful, often emotional closing ceremonies.

A Real Luau Buffet

Visitors wanting to feast on traditional Polynesian food may reserve a spot at the nightly Ali'i luau buffet. Watch the sundown Imu Ceremony in the Tongan village, where the succulent luau pig is removed from its lava-lined earthen oven, then relax and dine while watching a special luau show.

The Fabulous Buffets

Dinner is served in The Gateway Buffet Restaurant. Pink linen cloths and the Polynesian look create a perfect place to unwind after a day of adventuring. An opulent, unlimited buffet is spread out in three bounteous displays: a salad station, the main course array and a table of tempting desserts.

For those desiring an even more extravagant dining experience, the exclusive Ambassador Buffet features a menu of prime rib, shrimp scampi and a number of Japanese specialties such as sashimi and sushi. There is table service for beverages, and a quiet, sophisticated ambience.

As for the future? Well, come back and see what new delights the Polynesian Cultural Center is cooking up.
Come back soon to Polynesia.

"Aloha" means come back and good health until we meet again.

Come Along and Learn, If You Wish

The special Laie Tour goes by tram beyond the Polynesian Cultural Center through the historic Hawaiian community of Laie, the sprawling Brigham Young University Hawai'i and the beautiful grounds of the Mormon Temple. The free, optional 45-minute tour pauses at the Temple's Visitor Center and offers a film and an opportunity to learn more about The Church of Jesus Christ of Latter-day Saints.

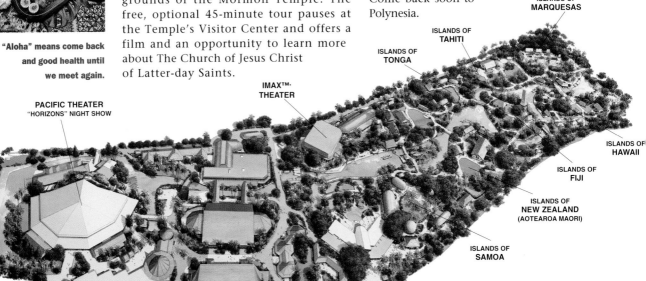

ISLANDS OF MARQUESAS

ISLANDS OF TAHITI

ISLANDS OF TONGA

ISLANDS OF HAWAII

ISLANDS OF FIJI

ISLANDS OF NEW ZEALAND (AOTEAROA MAORI)

ISLANDS OF SAMOA

IMAX™ THEATER

PACIFIC THEATER "HORIZONS" NIGHT SHOW